FAQ

TEEN LIFE™

FREQUENTLY ASKED QUESTIONS ABOUT

Tanning and Skin Care

Corona
Brezina

ROSEN
PUBLISHING®

New York

Published in 2010 by The Rosen Publishing Group, Inc.
29 East 21st Street, New York, NY 10010

Library of Congress Cataloging-in-Publication Data

Brezina, Corona.
Frequently asked questions about tanning and skin care / Corona Brezina.—1st ed.
    p. cm.—(FAQ: teen life)
Includes index.
ISBN 978-1-4358-3545-0 (library binding)
1. Skin—Care and hygiene—Popular works. 2. Skin—Cancer—Prevention—Popular works. 3. Suntan—Health aspects—Popular works. I. Title.
RL87.B715 2010
616.5—dc22

                                                    2009013653

Manufactured in Malaysia

CPSIA Compliance Information: Batch #TWW10YA: For Further Information contact Rosen Publishing, New York, New York at 1-800-237-9932

Contents

WHY IS TANNING SO POPULAR?

During the long, hot days of summer, beaches and pools are packed with swimmers and sunbathers with deep bronze tans. Summer is the time for sports, outdoor jobs, and other sun-soaked activities that give the skin a chance to acquire a tan. The price of this golden skin might be a sunburn early in the summer, but to many young people, that's no big deal.

Many adolescents and young adults, however, are no longer limiting their ultraviolet radiation (UVR) exposure to summertime hours in the sun. (UVR is the component of light from the sun that tans and burns the skin.) They are flocking to tanning salons, where they can get a tan year-round from tanning machines that expose the skin to UVR. Rather than resigning themselves to eight months of pale skin every year, young people may treat themselves to a few

After a stretch of cold and rainy weather, people head to the beach on a sunny summer day.

sessions of indoor tanning for special occasions, such as prom or going on vacation. Some tan regularly so that they never lose that golden color.

These trends in tanning are a huge concern for dermatologists—doctors who specialize in treating medical conditions affecting the skin—and other medical professionals. Increased UVR exposure increases the risk of skin cancer, and rates of skin cancer in the United States and worldwide have been rising. Tanning also causes wrinkles, weathering, and other signs of aging later in life. Health professionals warn over and over that there is no such thing as a safe tan. They are often frustrated that teens and young adults are aware of some of the risks of sun exposure but choose to tan anyway.

The Draws of Tanning

Today, tanning is not just a side effect of spending time outdoors. Teenagers set out to get a tan solely for cosmetic reasons. People tend to view tanned skin as healthy and attractive, and people usually feel healthier when they have a tan. Advertisements and photos of celebrities show beautiful, smiling people, often with glowing bronze skin. Many young people hang out with a crowd of friends who all tan. A teen might start out by getting a tan for a special occasion and then fall into a regular habit of tanning. Medical professionals emphasize the risks of tanning. But for many teens, a possibility of health complications far in the future is not an adequately compelling reason to give up the short-term satisfaction of deeply tanned skin.

About 10 percent of all Americans visit tanning salons every year—that's about thirty million people. Most customers are women.

There may be a secondary explanation for the popularity of tanning. Some studies have shown that tanning may be addictive in the same sense that drugs and alcohol are addictive. UVR exposure may cause the release of chemicals in the brain that elevate mood. In one study, 20 percent of tanners felt guilty about their tanning habits, and some tanners said they knew that tanning is unhealthy but didn't want to stop.

Trends in Tanning

Statistics confirm the popularity of tanning. Today, indoor tanning is a $5 billion-a-year industry. Every day, more than a million people visit tanning salons. Thirty million Americans tan indoors every year, including 2.3 million teenagers. Nearly three-quarters of the customers at tanning salons are women between the ages of sixteen and twenty-nine. One survey of adults under twenty-five years of age found that nearly 26 percent had visited a tanning salon in the past year. Another survey of college students found that 47 percent had tanned indoors in the past year.

Public awareness campaigns have not curbed the popularity of indoor tanning, nor have they convinced teens to adequately protect their skin from the rays of the sun. They are aware of the risks of tanning—80 percent say they know that it isn't healthy. Nevertheless, only about one-third of teenagers apply sunscreen on sunny days. (Dermatologists recommend that people use sunscreen year-round.) Most say they have been sunburned in the past year. Since UVR exposure and sunburn are risk factors for skin cancer, health professionals warn that young people might be gambling with their health just to get a tan.

Rising Rates of Skin Cancer

The U.S. Department of Health and Human Services and the World Health Organization (WHO) have both recognized that UVR is a carcinogen—an agent that directly causes cancer.

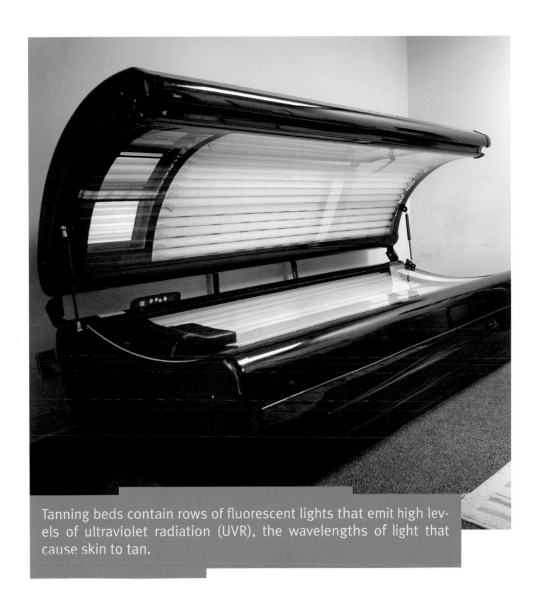

Tanning beds contain rows of fluorescent lights that emit high levels of ultraviolet radiation (UVR), the wavelengths of light that cause skin to tan.

Severe sunburns and excessive UVR exposure can cause damage that can lead to skin cancer. According to the Skin Cancer Foundation, more than a million cases of skin cancer are diagnosed annually in the United States, making it the most prevalent type of cancer. One in five Americans will be diagnosed with skin cancer. The two most common types of skin cancer—basal cell carcinoma (BCC) and squamous cell carcinoma (SCC)—can be cured when detected early. About 90 percent of all cases are linked to UVR exposure.

Rates of melanoma, sometimes called malignant melanoma, are also rising. Melanoma accounts for a small percentage of skin cancer cases, but it is the deadliest form of the disease. Every year, more than eight thousand people in the United States die of melanoma. Skin cancer used to be a disease of the middle aged and elderly, but more and more young people are being diagnosed with melanoma. It is now the second most common form of cancer among people between the ages of fifteen and twenty-nine. Studies have shown that UVR exposure increases the risk of developing melanoma, although the link is not as direct as with BCC and SCC.

Tanning salon owners try to downplay the link between UVR and skin cancer. They often claim, misleadingly, that the UVR produced by tanning machines is "healthier" than sunlight. In reality, people who tan indoors are 1.5 times more likely to develop BCC and 2.5 times more likely to develop SCC. Using a tanning bed just once raises the risk of melanoma 75 percent in young people.

Legislating Indoor Tanning

Skin cancer rates have become a matter of concern for some lawmakers as well as health organizations. In 1994, the

American Medical Association (AMA) and the American Academy of Dermatology (AAD) recommended that the U.S. Food and Drug Administration (FDA) ban indoor tanning. More recently, the WHO advised that people under eighteen years old should not use tanning machines at all.

About twenty state legislatures in the United States have passed laws that are intended to curb indoor tanning by teens. Many states require parental consent before teens can use tanning machines. A 2008 survey, however, showed that passing laws to discourage teen tanning had little effect on their tanning habits.

WHAT ARE SOME TYPICAL TANNING PRACTICES?

Most health professionals stand by the statement that there is no such thing as a healthy tan. In general, they do not approve of the habits of serious tanners who spend long hours in the sun. Both tanners and doctors agree on one point, however: it is important to take steps to avoid getting sunburned.

Suntans and sunburns both result from chemical reactions in the skin caused by a component of sunlight. The sun produces different wavelengths of radiation, including visible light and ultraviolet radiation (UVR). UVR is the type of radiation that affects the skin. UVR consists of several different wavelengths, including UVA, UVB, and UVC. UVC and 90 percent of UVB rays are filtered out by ozone and oxygen in Earth's atmosphere. UVA and 10 percent of UVB rays pass through the atmosphere to Earth's surface. In general, about 95 percent of all UVR is UVA, while 5 percent is UVB.

During the 1970s, scientists became aware that pollution caused by human activity was damaging Earth's ozone layer. They found that levels of ozone in the upper atmosphere of the planet were dropping and that there was a massive area of depletion—the ozone hole—over Antarctica. The thinning of the ozone layer allows more UVB to reach Earth's surface than in the past.

Common-sense measures can protect the skin and eyes from sun damage. During peak hours of UVR levels, it's a good idea to stay indoors or seek shade.

Overall levels of UVR vary, depending on such factors as geographic location, the season of the year, climate, altitude, and the time of day. UVR levels are measured on a scale called the UV index. At the lowest levels, 2 or less, there is little danger to the skin from sun exposure. At moderate levels, such as 5, people should protect themselves from sun exposure with sunscreen, a hat, and sunglasses. At very high and extreme levels—8 to 11+ on the scale—people should take great care to protect themselves from the sun and try to minimize sun exposure. UV index levels for different geographic regions can be found on the Internet, and they are reported daily by some newspapers and TV stations as part of the weather forecast.

The UV index can be a valuable resource for people who work outdoors and cannot avoid sun exposure. It can also be useful in planning outdoors activities, such as yard work, sports events, or a trip to the beach.

Worshipping the Sun

Despite warnings by dermatologists and other health experts, there are still plenty of people who head outdoors on sunny summer days to bake themselves in the sun. Many sun worshippers have established routines for sunning themselves. They aim to develop the richest tan possible but avoid burning their skin. They often change position to expose every area of the body and develop an even tan. They take care to keep their swimwear from slipping so that they have pronounced dark tan lines.

Some of the steps they take make good sense for skin health. For example, they may regularly exfoliate their skin to remove the layer of dead skin cells. They moisturize to keep the skin from drying out due to sun exposure. While tanning, they drink plenty of water to keep the body and skin hydrated. Most serious tanners also apply suntan lotion that provides some screening from the sun, but at a lower level of protection than that recommended by health experts. This protects them from burning and allows the skin to develop a tan more slowly.

A deep tan requires long hours spent in the sun, but sun worshippers aiming for the richest tan generally restrict the time of each session in order to avoid burning. They limit themselves to an hour or two in the sun every day or every other day. Both suntans and sunburns take time to develop, so it is not possible to determine how the sun has affected skin until hours afterward. More important, the serious effects of suntans and burns may not be seen until many years later, when the damage is irreversible.

Indoor Tanning

Despite warnings by health experts about the dangers of overexposure to UVR, many people still pay for the service at tanning salons. Tanning beds and booths tan the body through UVR emitted by fluorescent lamps. People may opt for a "fake bake" for a variety of reasons. They may wish to acquire a tan for a special event, such as prom or a wedding. They may want to get an early start on tanning for the summer. Some people may wish to keep their tan year-round.

Since UVR emissions vary from one tanning bed to another, the FDA requires that salons post a "recommended exposure schedule" for each unit.

Most people who tan indoors use tanning beds. The client lies on the bed, which exposes the skin to light on all sides. Goggles or other eye protection are required to prevent damage to the eyes; clothing is optional. Usually, the salon operator limits the session length for first-time clients. If the client does not burn, sessions are subsequently extended by two minutes. Typically, people who maintain a deep tan use a tanning bed three times weekly for sessions typically lasting about twenty minutes. Some beds have stronger lamps, which shorten the session length. Many salons have fans circulating air through the beds. After a tanning session, clients often notice an unpleasant burnt odor on their skin.

Some people choose to use a tanning booth, in which they tan standing up, rather than a tanning bed. This is largely a matter of personal preference, since both methods involve lamps that emit UVR. People may prefer tanning booths because they believe they are more sanitary. (This is not necessarily true—tanning bed operators generally disinfect units after each use.) Some people think booths provide a more even tan, since they can hold onto overhead handles in order to tan the underside of their arms. For some individuals, using a tanning bed results in a slight unevenness in the tan at the areas of skin that are in contact with the bed. Tanning in a booth eliminates this side effect.

There are similarities and differences between the tanning experience in a salon and tanning in sunlight. Whether the source is a lightbulb or the sun, UVR causes the skin to tan through the same chemical and biological processes. In both cases, it takes time before the full effects of UVR exposure become apparent. The UVR in tanning salons, however, is not identical to sunlight. The proportions of UVA and UVB in these salons are different from the proportions in sunlight and may vary from one machine to another. Also, the UVR produced by tanning machines is much stronger and more intense than sunlight. According to the Skin Cancer Foundation, some tanning units emit UVA at levels twelve times stronger than sunlight. This is why a single session on a tanning bed is the equivalent of spending an entire day in the sun.

Use a sunscreen with a sun protection factor (SPF) of 15 or higher if you're going to spend time in the sun—and apply it liberally and frequently.

Many tanning salons attempt to dismiss the dangers of UVR, often with confusing and misleading information. They claim that tanning is safe, UVR in salons is healthier than sunlight, and there are benefits to UVR exposure. They even try to deny the health links between skin cancer and UVR exposure.

Sunless Tanning

Some people want bronzed skin but prefer to avoid UVR exposure. They may choose sunless self-tanners, such as tanning lotions, gels, and creams that can be used at home. In addition, salons offer professional sprays or airbrush applications of sunless tanning products.

The active ingredient in self-tanners is a chemical called dihydroxyacetone (DHA). DHA does not merely coat or stain the skin—it produces a chemical reaction on the surface layer of the skin. This interaction with components of the skin produces an effect that resembles a natural tan. The chemical reaction is not the same reaction that occurs during natural tanning, and sunless tanners do not require any UVR exposure in order to work effectively.

DHA is considered a safe cosmetic chemical by the FDA. Some people may be sensitive to the ingredient, however, or may have an allergic reaction to another ingredient in the formula. It is always a good idea to test a patch of skin the day before a full application. This is also a chance to check how the color develops.

In the past, self-tanners got a reputation for producing a bad imitation of a real tan, sometimes appearing blotchy, streaked, or orange-colored. The newest products, however, can create a smooth, realistic tan when properly applied. If you decide to try out a self-tanner, follow the directions on the product and look up tips on the Internet on how to get the best results.

Applying a sunless tanner is easy, but you'll get better results if you take the time to do a thorough and careful job. Again, be sure to read the directions. Some products are not intended for use on the face, so you may have to use two different types of lotions: one for the body and one for the face. Before beginning, exfoliate, clean, and dry your skin. Using your hands, evenly spread the tanning product over the skin. Wash your hands thoroughly every five minutes while applying—especially under and around the nails—or wear disposable gloves for the process. You must wait fifteen to thirty minutes for the lotion to dry, and it is a good idea to wear loose clothing for an additional hour afterward to avoid chafing the skin. The tanner may also stain your clothing. The color will take at least three hours to develop, and full color may not appear for as long as twenty-four hours.

The process for a sunless tan applied in a salon is similar, except the product is misted, airbrushed, or sprayed onto the skin. Avoid getting the product in the eyes, nose, or mouth. You may wish to wear eye protection and noseplugs when the product is being applied. A sunless tan generally lasts five to seven days. Self-tanners do not provide effective protection from the sun, so don't forget to apply sunscreen when you go outside.

In addition to sunless tanners containing DHA, there are various other products available that claim to produce or enhance a tan. Many of these products are ineffective or unsafe, and they may contain chemicals that are not approved by the FDA for cosmetic purposes. Two of the most common types are tanning accelerators and tanning pills. Tanning accelerators, sold as lotions or pills, claim to cause the skin to tan more quickly when exposed to UVR. Tanning pills affect the coloration of the skin without UVR exposure. These often contain a chemical called canthaxanthin that is deposited under the skin and causes a color change. Canthaxanthin is used as a food additive, but it is not approved for sunless tanning. It can cause serious side effects that can impact the eyes, liver, and skin.

Ten Great Questions to Ask a Dermatologist

1 I know that UVR has been proven to increase the risk of cancer, but the tanning salon claims to use only "healthy" forms of UVR. What's the truth of the matter?

2 Is sunless tanning, such as tanning lotions or spray-on tans, a safe alternative to UVR exposure?

3 How should I protect my skin from the sun when I go outdoors?

4 Where can I look up the UV index for my area?

5 What should I look for on the label when I'm picking out a sunscreen?

6 What's the best way to treat a serious sunburn?

7 How can I ensure that I get enough vitamin D?

8 Does my skin type, family history, lifestyle, or other factor put me at risk for skin cancer?

9 I have a couple of large moles or freckled skin. Should I be concerned about developing skin cancer?

10 How do I perform a self-examination for skin cancer?

HOW DOES TANNING AFFECT THE SKIN?

Explaining the effects of sunlight on the skin should be easy. Moderate exposure to the sun causes the skin to tan. Overexposure causes sunburn. Upon closer examination, though, the matter becomes more complicated. Some people have skin that burns easily or never tans. Sun exposure at midday during the summer may quickly burn the skin, while exposure during the evening has less of an effect. Most people worry about sun exposure during the summer, but skiers may get a sunburn on a sunny winter day. Some people hope that a tan will hide acne and blemishes on their complexion, while others believe that the health risks are worse than the temporary camouflage. Then there is the link between sun exposure and skin cancer. Health experts advise that protection from sun exposure is a common-sense prevention measure against skin cancer. Most people, however, do not know much about how cancer develops in the skin and might not recognize signs of skin cancer.

Skin Deep

To fully understand the short-term and long-term effects of sun exposure, it helps to know the basic structure and various

A cutaway illustration reveals the different layers of the skin, as well as constituent components that include hair follicles, blood vessels, nerve endings, and glands.

functions of the skin. The skin acts as a protective sheath that shields the organs, bones, and blood from injury, whether from UVR, heat, cold, infection, or physical damage. It helps regulate the temperature and fluid levels of the body. The skin is also a sensory organ that perceives touch, temperature, and pain. In addition, it produces vitamin D in response to sunlight.

The skin is the largest organ of the human body, making up about 15 percent of a person's total body weight. It consists of an area of 12 to 20 square feet (1.11 to 1.85 square meters). The skin also includes hair and hair follicles, fingernails and toenails, glands, and nerves.

Each layer of the skin has different properties and serves different functions. The outer layer of the skin is called the epidermis. It is slightly more than $1/32$ of an inch (about 1 millimeter) thick, and the dead cells that make up the top layer are constantly shedding and being replaced with new cells from below. The epidermis resists water, microorganisms, some chemicals, UVR, and other potentially harmful elements. If the epidermis is under stress, such as by repeated exposure to UVR, it can defend itself by becoming thicker.

The next layer of the skin is the dermis. This is the thickest layer of the skin, with an average thickness of 0.07 inches (2 mm). The dermis protects the body from physical injuries, such as cuts and impacts. It also contains blood vessels, sweat and oil glands, hair follicles, nerve endings, lymph nodes, and some muscle cells. The dermis is tough, elastic, and resilient. It largely consists of a protein called collagen interwoven with filaments of another protein called elastin. Collagen and elastin deteriorate with age, and they are susceptible to irreversible damage by UVR.

The third layer of the skin is the subcutis, or subcutaneous tissue. It consists of fat and acts as an insulator and energy reservoir in the body.

The Skin's Response to UVR

The deepest sublayer of the epidermis contains cells called melanocytes. These special cells produce melanin, a dark brown skin pigment. In general, everybody has the same number of melanocytes in their skin. The activity of the melanocytes, however, varies greatly from one skin type to

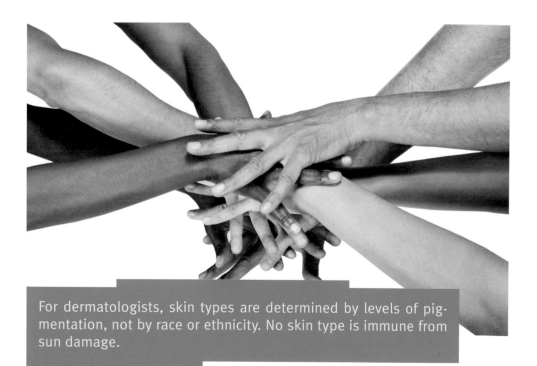

For dermatologists, skin types are determined by levels of pigmentation, not by race or ethnicity. No skin type is immune from sun damage.

another. For people with darker skin, their melanocytes produce more melanin, and the size of each pigment granule is larger. For people with lighter skin, their melanocytes produce a lesser amount of melanin. Melanin production also varies with age. Children have fewer active melanocytes, and melanin production increases as teens reach puberty—this is why protection from UVR exposure is particularly crucial for young children. For adults, levels of melanin production drop after the age of thirty-five.

A tan occurs when UVR exposure darkens existing melanin and stimulates further melanin production in the skin. Melanin production is a gradual process—it takes time to build up melanin levels. Depending on the activity of an individual's melanocytes, repeated UVR exposure may result in a deep bronze tan or may bring about very little change in skin tone. Tanning is a result of exposure to both wavelengths—UVA and UVB.

Shorter wavelengths of light cause greater damage to the skin than longer wavelengths. UVB, which is shorter than UVA, is the wavelength primarily responsible for sunburn. Sunburn manifests as redness of the skin due to increased blood flow. A sunburn begins with initial redness that lasts only as long as the UVR exposure. A bad sunburn develops as a delayed reaction a few hours after exposure and peaks within twenty-four hours. The symptoms of sunburn, such as redness, swelling, fever, pain, blistering, and peeling, are a result of the damage done by UVR exposure and the body's reaction. In some very severe cases, people have died from overexposure to UVR.

Skin Type

Skin tone varies greatly from one individual to another due to different levels and types of pigmentation. In general, most dark-skinned people had ancestors who lived near the equator or in other parts of the world with high UVR levels. The ancestors of light-skinned people came from northern regions that received lower levels of UVR. Natural skin pigmentation determines both sensitivity to UVR exposure and the ability to synthesize vitamin D from sunlight.

In determining risk for skin cancer, doctors classify skin tone into six types. These classifications are called phototypes because they identify a person's likely reaction to UVR. People who have darker pigmentation prior to UVR exposure have more natural protection. UVR exposure is assumed to be a half hour in the sun at midday, midsummer levels.

Phototype	Skin Tone	Reaction to UVR Exposure
I	Pale white	Always sunburns, never tans
II	Pale white/white	Sunburns, tans minimally
III	White	Sunburns moderately, tans moderately
IV	Light brown/beige	Sunburns minimally, tans moderately
V	Moderate brown	Rarely sunburns, tans to dark brown
VI	Dark brown/black	Does not burn

People who have phototypes I and II are said to be melano-compromised; types II and IV are melano-competent; and types V and VI are melano-protected. These terms describe the natural levels of pigmentation in the skin. The group most at risk for skin cancer are Caucasians with pale skin, blond or red hair, and light eyes.

Are There Physical Benefits to Tanning?

Tanning salons often state that tanning is healthy. They even claim that UVR emitted in tanning machines is healthier than UVR from sunlight. In reality, excessive UVR exposure damages the skin, no matter what the source. The health claims by the indoor tanning industry are misleading. For example, when describing the health benefits of UVB, a FAQ page of the Indoor Tanning Association's Web site quoted data from a 1941 magazine article—information that's seventy years out of date.

Nonetheless, it is true that there are some health benefits of mild UVR exposure. The most crucial effect is the activation of vitamin D in the body. Exposure to UVB causes the formation of a molecule called vitamin D_3 in the epidermis and dermis. Processes in the liver and kidneys convert vitamin D_3 into vitamin D, the form that the body can utilize.

Vitamin D regulates levels of calcium and phosphorus in the blood. The lack of it can prevent proper absorption of calcium from food. Since calcium is the primary building block of the skeleton, a childhood vitamin D deficiency can have devastating consequences. The most severe condition caused by vitamin D deficiency is rickets, a disease characterized by soft bones (decreased mineralization). This can lead to weak, bowed legs.

Studies have shown that sun exposure can reduce the risk of some cancers—such as prostate cancer, breast cancer, and lung

Egg yolks—along with fish, cheese, and beef liver—are among the few foods that naturally contain vitamin D. Milk and some foods are fortified with vitamin D.

cancer—and some autoimmune conditions, such as multiple sclerosis. It can be an important treatment for some autoimmune skin conditions. Scientists believe that the reason is the stimulation of vitamin D production by UVR. Research in the lab has also shown that vitamin D can halt the growth of tumors.

In general, ten to twenty minutes of daily sun exposure during off-peak hours can provide more than enough vitamin D. Sunscreen blocks UVB. Some sources advise protecting the face and hands with a hat and sunscreen while allowing about 40 percent of the body to be exposed to the sun. Indoor tanning is not a safe substitute, since the levels of UVR produced by tanning machines far exceed the moderate levels necessary for vitamin D production.

Other experts, however, believe that the risks of sun exposure outweigh the benefits. Vitamin D can also be obtained from the diet. Egg yolks, some fish, and vitamin D–fortified milk all contain good amounts of vitamin D. Vitamin D supplements are also available, although consumers should be aware that extremely large doses of vitamin D can cause health problems.

People with dark skin tones and those who live at northern latitudes are at a higher risk for vitamin D deficiency. Dark skin offers natural protection from the sunlight, but this protection reduces the ability to synthesize vitamin D from UVR. Dark skin can take more than five times as long as lighter skin to attain the same level of vitamin D. This is an issue of concern particularly in northern latitudes, where the atmosphere filters out more of the UVB and there is generally less sunlight, especially in the winter.

Myths and Facts

Using a tanning bed can reduce seasonal affective disorder (SAD) in the winter.

FACT: ➡ During winter months, some people suffer from seasonal affective disorder, sometimes known as winter depression. The primary treatment for SAD is light therapy, usually utilizing a specialized light box that mimics outdoor light. Tanning salons sometimes advertise tanning machines as a remedy for SAD. Tanning under UV light, however, is not an appropriate or effective treatment.

A base tan works as a natural sunscreen and protects from sunburn and skin cancer.

FACT: ➡ A base tan provides protection equivalent to only SPF 3 to 5. Since a tan is evidence of UVR damage to the skin, the health risks involved in acquiring a base tan are not worth the slight level of sun protection it provides.

Myth

I don't have to worry about skin cancer or the effects of sun exposure because I have naturally dark skin.

FACT: ➡ Dark skin provides a natural sunscreen that is about twice as effective at screening out UVR as light skin. Still, UVR stimulates the skin—light or dark—to increase melanin production, and UVR overexposure will lead to sunburn. According to the Skin Cancer Foundation, Asian Americans and African Americans with melanoma are more likely to be diagnosed at a later stage of the disease. The overall survival rate for African Americans with melanoma is 77 percent, while it is 91 percent for Caucasians. For people with dark skin, skin cancer tends to occur on the palms of the hands, the soles of the feet, and around the nails.

Four

WHAT ARE THE LONG-TERM EFFECTS OF TANNING?

Flawless skin, tanned or not, doesn't last forever. Wrinkles, age spots, and other outward signs of aging are a natural part of growing older. Lifestyle choices can affect this aging process. Smoking, for example, accelerates wrinkling and causes the skin to turn leathery. Some sleeping positions can eventually lead to permanent "sleep lines." The worst culprit for aging skin prematurely, however, is UVR exposure.

The technical term for aging caused by UVR is "photoaging." UVA, which penetrates the skin more deeply than UVB, is responsible for most of the damage. It penetrates the dermis and breaks down the collagen and elastin. The enzymes that build skin occasionally make errors in repairing the damage, resulting in a weathered appearance over time. After

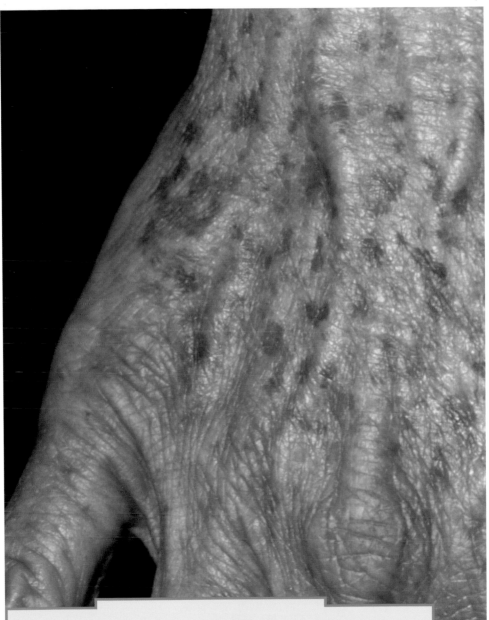

Sun exposure is one of the contributing factors to the development of lentigos, also called age spots or liver spots. Although generally benign, lentigos can occasionally turn cancerous.

longtime overexposure to UVR, the skin is no longer able to repair itself as efficiently.

This damage causes a loss of elasticity in the skin, leading to wrinkles and lines. UVR exposure also affects the pigment and texture of the skin. Liver spots accumulate, particularly on the hands, arms, and face. The skin becomes loose and thinner. It becomes drier and rougher. Some people develop actinic keratoses—scaly patches of rough, reddened skin—that can turn into squamous cell cancers if left untreated. Other signs of photoaging include freckling, red broken veins, and a mottled complexion.

Skin damage inflicted by UVR is cumulative. Every minute of exposure, whether it's a fifteen-minute walk to the store on a sunny day or a long session in a tanning bed, impacts the skin. You can't reverse the effects of UVR exposure. The best you can do is practice sensible sun protection in the future.

It's difficult for young people to gauge sun damage to their skin because the effects typically do not appear for years or even decades. UV light cameras can be used to detect underlying damage from the sun that is not yet apparent to the naked eye. Teenagers and adults in their twenties may show evidence of significant damage under the skin. Even children may exhibit freckling from the sun in a UV photograph.

Deeper Damage

Overexposure to UVR causes damage beyond what is visible on the surface. UVR can also damage the DNA in the skin. This

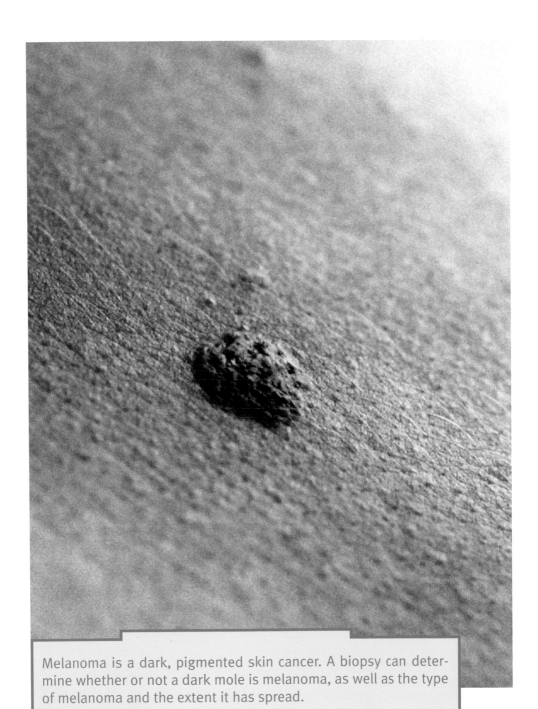

Melanoma is a dark, pigmented skin cancer. A biopsy can determine whether or not a dark mole is melanoma, as well as the type of melanoma and the extent it has spread.

occurs when UVR causes mutations in DNA that change the chemical composition of the molecule. The body has mechanisms to repair DNA damage, but there are occasional errors that result in defective DNA. The cumulative effects of sun exposure increase the amount of faulty DNA in the skin. Since DNA is involved with the repair and regeneration of the skin, damaged DNA can result in abnormal skin cells. These cells may die, or they could begin to grow and spread. This uncontrolled growth of abnormal cells is one cause of skin cancer.

It was long believed that UVB was the cancer-causing range of the UV spectrum. Recent research, however, has shown that UVA also causes damage to DNA linked with skin cancer. UVB causes direct damage in the surface layers of the skin. UVA can damage the lower layers of the skin, where skin cancers originate. It may contribute to cancer—including the most severe form, malignant melanoma—through indirect damage to DNA. This occurs when UVA exposure triggers the formation of damaging particles, such as free radicals in the skin.

UVR may also cause deficiencies in some vitamins in the body, such as folate and vitamin A. Since folate is essential for the healthy development of a fetus, pregnant women should avoid UVR overexposure. UVR has also been shown to suppress the immune system. This can make it more difficult for the body to respond to infection or fight cancer.

Detecting Melanoma

Many people have moles on their skin, and most moles are normal and benign. They are caused by a cluster of melanocytes

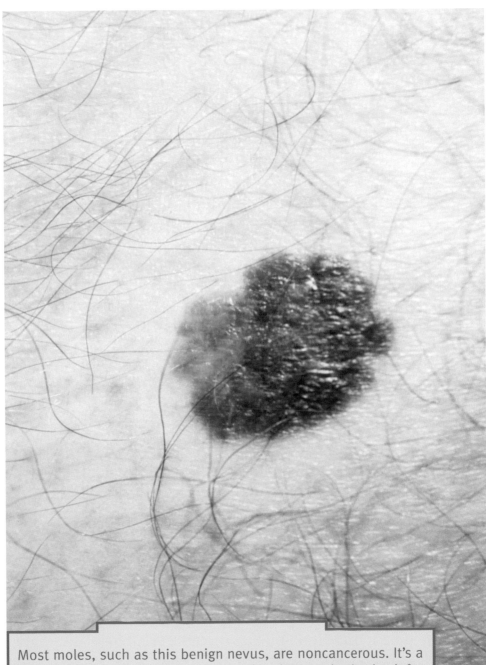

Most moles, such as this benign nevus, are noncancerous. It's a good idea to occasionally perform a head-to-toe body check for skin changes.

beneath the skin. Moles (the scientific name for a mole is *nevus*; plural *nevi*) typically have moderate-to-dark pigmentation and smooth edges. People may tend to develop more moles as they grow older. Risk factors for melanoma include a large number of moles on the skin or more than four abnormally large moles having light skin, and/or a family history of melanoma.

An atypical mole may be an indication of melanoma, especially when the mole has changed in appearance. There is an "ABCD" method of evaluating whether or not a mole could be a matter of concern:

A—Asymmetry	The halves of the mole are not mirror images.
B—Border Irregularity	The edges of the mole are irregular or notched in shape.
C—Color	The color is not uniform—it may appear black, brown, green, or tan; it might be mottled with red, blue, or white.
D—Diameter	It is larger in size than a pencil eraser.

Also, a mole that itches, bleeds, or burns should be checked out immediately by a doctor.

Melanoma most often appears on the back, chest, abdomen, or legs. It may also appear on parts of the body that are not typically exposed to the sun, such as beneath the fingernails. Melanoma often develops from existing moles.

When a doctor encounters an abnormal mole, he or she may recommend a biopsy. A biopsy is a tissue sample taken for medical evaluation. In dealing with melanoma, an entire mole or just a portion of the mole may be removed during the biopsy. The biopsy is then sent to a pathologist, a doctor who will evaluate the sample after examining it under a microscope.

Diagnosing and Treating Melanoma

The pathologist will determine whether the mole was actually a melanoma or is at risk of becoming a melanoma. If the diagnosis is melanoma, the pathologist will evaluate such factors as the type and invasiveness of the cancer.

After a diagnosis, the patient undergoes a series of tests called staging to determine how far the cancer has progressed. About 95 percent of melanoma cases can be cured if caught early, but this cancer can be quickly fatal if it has spread to other parts of the body. When melanoma is detected early in its development, it is stage I, the stage with the highest rate of survival. Stage I cancer is the least invasive and occurs in the top layers of the skin. Stage II cancer penetrates slightly deeper into the dermis. Stage III cancer extends to the lymph nodes surrounding the mole. (Lymph nodes are part of the immune system.) Stage IV cancer affects multiple parts of the body and may include internal organs of the body, as well as the skin and lymph nodes. Workup of stage III and IV cancers is extensive and may include

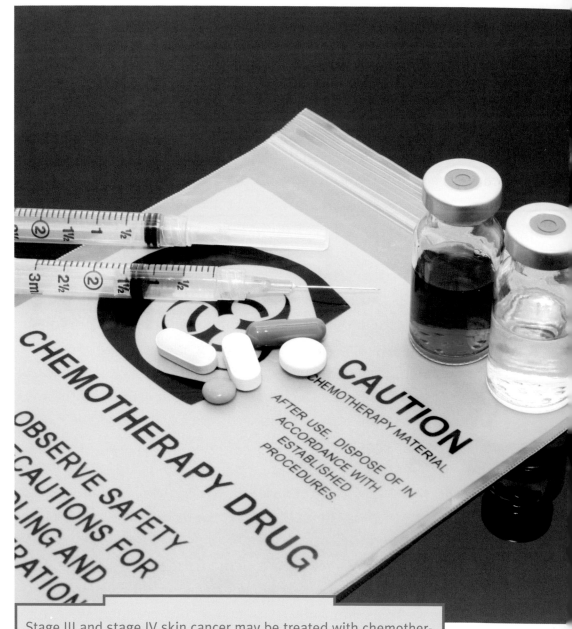

Stage III and stage IV skin cancer may be treated with chemotherapy, a drug treatment that kills cancerous cells but also kills some normal cells of the body.

advanced scans of the organs, bones, brain, and full body. Patients with advanced melanoma are usually referred to a doctor called an oncologist, which is a cancer specialist for chemotherapy or other treatments.

Treatment of melanoma varies depending on the stage. Following the initial biopsy, a specially trained dermatologist may remove tissue around the melanoma to ensure that all of the cancerous cells are gone. If doctors believe that the lymph nodes are affected, a surgeon may perform a biopsy of one or more lymph nodes and evaluate the sample. The surgeon may recommend having more extensive surgery on the lymph nodes. Stage III cancer may also require adjuvant therapy, which is treatment that will prevent any recurrence of melanoma. A few forms of adjuvant therapy are immunotherapy, chemotherapy, and radiation. Immunotherapy uses special chemicals and antibodies to fight cancer. Chemotherapy drugs are used to kill cancer cells. Radiation, which is less commonly used for adjuvant therapy in treating melanoma, kills the cancer cells with radiation waves.

A stage IV diagnosis means that cancer has spread to other sites in the body—often the lungs, liver, or brain. It can, however, invade and form tumors in any organ in the body. Some patients respond to treatment, but only about 5 percent are cured in the long term. In general, organ deterioration and failure leads to death in a matter of months or a couple of years. Stage IV melanoma is typically treated through surgery, immunotherapy, chemotherapy, and radiation. Some patients may choose to participate in clinical trials, which test new experimental drugs.

Non-melanoma Skin Cancers

Melanoma is the most notorious and deadly form of skin cancer. But according to the American Academy of Dermatology (AAD), it makes up only about 4 percent of skin cancer cases. There are two other types of commonly diagnosed skin cancer. Eighty percent of all cases are basal cell carcinoma (BCC), and about 16 percent are squamous cell carcinoma (SCC). These forms of skin cancer are generally easy to treat when detected early. Rarer forms of skin cancer account for less than 1 percent of all cases.

BCC and SCC are sometimes called non-pigmented skin cancers. Most cases appear in areas of the skin that have received high levels of UVR exposure. Research has shown that exposure to UVB, which damages the upper layers of the skin, increases the risk of these types of skin cancer. BCCs and SCCs are not related to melanoma, and they cannot develop into melanoma.

A BCC may appear as a raised pink-to-reddish bump with a pearly sheen, often with tiny, visible blood vessels near the surface. Sometimes, it resembles a volcano because it can have a depressed middle part. BCCs frequently occur on the face and head—especially on the nose and the tops of the ears—and on the shoulders or back. They are generally removed surgically and are biopsied, though they may be treated by nonsurgical methods, such as drugs that are applied to the skin. BCCs grow slowly and rarely spread to other parts of the body.

SCCs occur on the same sun-exposed areas of the body as BCCs, but they tend to look somewhat different. They tend to be flatter and have a rough or crusted surface, and they are likelier to break open and bleed. Like BCCs, SCCs are generally removed surgically. SCCs grow more quickly and are slightly more prone to spread to the lymph nodes or other parts of the body. In some cases, they may recur or cause disfiguration around the area of occurrence. Still, if an SCC is detected and treated early in its development, it can generally be cured with a low risk of complications or damage to the skin. Actinic keratoses, caused by sun damage, can develop into SCCs if left untreated.

WHAT DO DOCTORS SAY ABOUT TANNING?

Many people, especially young adults, view a tan as a mark of health and beauty. For medical professionals, however, a tan is evidence of injury to the skin. The skin develops a tan in the upper layers in order to keep UVR from penetrating and causing damage to the deeper layers of the skin.

Despite public awareness efforts by health organizations, tanning remains popular. Many people do not adequately protect themselves from the sun. Rates of many kinds of cancer are falling, but skin cancer rates are rising.

The AAD has referred to skin cancer as an "unrecognized epidemic." Dermatologists also caution people about the photoaging that will eventually result from overexposure to UVR. A suntan might give the appearance of radiant good health, but it can eventually lead to health consequences and visible damage. Health professionals advise people to avoid indoor tanning and take routine protective measures from the sun.

Saving Your Skin

Common-sense skin protection starts with a healthy respect for the sun's rays. Many people don't bother with sunscreen unless they're planning to spend a day on the beach in the full sun. Most experts, however, advise people to avoid spending time outdoors or to seek shade when the sun is most intense. This is generally between 10 AM and 4 PM during the summer. People who live at higher altitudes or closer to the equator need to take even more care to protect their skin. It's no coincidence that many cultures in hot climates developed a tradition of an afternoon siesta.

You might not think that sun exposure would be an issue indoors, on cloudy days, or during the winter. But dermatologists disagree. Glass blocks UVB, but it does not stop UVA. Likewise, UVB is blocked by cloud cover, but UVA penetrates clouds. Snow and ice—as well as water and sand—reflect almost 80 percent of UVB rays. Skiers and other winter athletes are therefore exposed to nearly a double dose of UVB because of the reflected radiation. The high altitude of many slopes also increases the levels of UVB.

Many people do not use enough sunscreen to adequately protect the skin. Sunscreen should be applied fifteen to thirty minutes before sun exposure. For most people planning to

Most people do not apply enough sunscreen. If you only use half as much sunscreen as you should, it will reduce the sun protection level by half.

spend time outdoors in a bathing suit, 1 ounce (about 2 table-spoons) is the amount of lotion needed to cover the body. It should be reapplied every two hours, or after swimming, tow-eling off, or sweating heavily. Be thorough—don't neglect areas like the ears, neck, skin underneath the chin, and scalp. The lips can also sunburn, so it is a good idea to apply a lip balm with sun protection. Lipstick does not provide adequate protection.

There is a difference between sunblock and sunscreen. Sunblock, which contains chemicals like zinc oxide, provides a physical barrier that reflects the sunlight so that it does not reach the surface of the skin. It is sometimes visible when applied to the skin. Sunscreen absorbs the energy from UVR, preventing it from damaging the skin. Many products labeled "sunscreen" also have ingredients that physically block the sun.

The level of sun protection in sunscreens is measured by the sun protection factor (SPF) scale. The SPF number indicates the extent that the sunscreen filters out UVB rays. Most derma-tologists advise using a sunscreen with SPF 15 or higher. A sunscreen with SPF 15 screens out 93 percent of UVB rays. A sun-screen with SPF 50 screens out 98 percent. The SPF rating does not measure protection against UVA. Choose a sunscreen labeled "broad protection" or "broad spectrum," since this prod-uct will also contain ingredients that block UVA.

Some people dislike wearing sunscreen because it feels sticky or causes their skin to break out. That's not a good excuse, since there are a variety of oil-free products, moisturiz-ing lotions, and other sunscreen options. Sunscreen is available in such forms as gels, creams, sticks, and sprays. All varieties are effective.

Finally, health experts advise people to cover up with a long-sleeved shirt, long pants, a broad-brimmed hat, and sunglasses. Dark clothing with a tight weave offers the most protection, since light-colored T-shirts or loose-weave fabrics allow UVR to pass through. The type of material also makes a difference— polyester, for example, tends to reflect UVR. Some companies sell sun-protective clothing that covers as much skin as possible and prevents UVR penetration. Just as sunscreens are rated by SPF numbers, clothing can be rated on the ultraviolet protection factor, or UPF, system. A hat should have a brim wide enough to shade the neck, face, and ears.

Sunglasses protect the eyes as well as the sensitive skin around the eyes, which can be a difficult area to cover thoroughly with sunscreen. Basal cell carcinoma and squamous cell carcinoma can both occur on the eyelids and nearby skin. There is also a form of melanoma called ocular melanoma that affects the eye itself. In addition, UVR can damage the eyes directly, increasing the risk of such conditions as cataracts. Most sunglasses block both UVA and UVB, but it's still a good idea to check the label for details on sun protection.

Medical Considerations

Some people are particularly vulnerable to damage from UVR. Some albinos, for example, cannot produce melanin in the skin or hair. They are highly susceptible to sunburn and skin cancer.

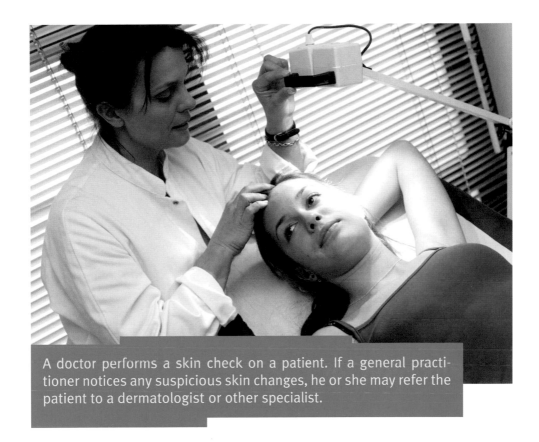

A doctor performs a skin check on a patient. If a general practitioner notices any suspicious skin changes, he or she may refer the patient to a dermatologist or other specialist.

People who are photosensitive experience an abnormal skin reaction when exposed to UVR. This can range from a mild rash to damage resembling sunburn to extreme blistering. Photosensitivity may be caused by medical conditions, such as lupus (an autoimmune disease) or the porphyrias (a group of disorders that affects the skin and nervous system).

Photosensitive reactions can also result as a side effect of some drugs, medications, and other substances, either from ingestion or contact with the skin. Certain foods, such as celery and limes, can even cause photosensitization in some people upon contact with the skin. If you are taking a prescription or over-the-counter drug, you should check if it can cause photo-sensitivity. Many people who experience photosensitive responses do not realize it, believing that the skin reaction was sunburn or a rash brought on by another cause.

Some medical conditions are treated by UV exposure. When used therapeutically, UV and other light exposure are called phototherapy. Phototherapy is also sometimes used to treat psoriasis and vitiligo, two skin diseases. UV exposure used for medical purposes may put patients at an increased risk of developing skin cancer, so it should only be done under a dermatologist's supervision.

Healthy Skin for Life

If you absolutely must have a tan, dermatologists recommend that you use a sunless tanner. On the other hand, there are plenty of ways that you can bring out the beauty in your skin without tanning. Making good skin care choices can help your skin stay radiant for a lifetime.

Many decisions that promote an overall healthy lifestyle also benefit the skin. Don't smoke, as smoking affects the blood cir-culation in the skin and deprives the skin of nutrients, aging the skin. Eat a healthy diet with plenty of fruits, vegetables, and whole grains. Avoid saturated and trans fats, which raise the levels of fat in the blood and, in turn, negatively affect the skin. Many dermatologists tell people to limit the amount of sugar

No matter what your skin type, making good diet and other lifestyle decisions—including sun protection—can improve your skin health.

they consume. In addition, some foods contain particular nutrients that benefit the skin. Blueberries, strawberries, and some other fruits contain antioxidants. Foods like salmon, nuts, and flaxseed contain essential fatty acids, such as DHA-omega-3. The compounds in green tea may help reduce the damage caused by UVR exposure.

A regular skin care routine can improve the everyday appearance of your skin. Choose products for your skin type—normal, oily, dry, sensitive, or combination. Skin care products don't need to be expensive to be effective. Start with a gentle soap or cleanser. Stronger soaps may leave your skin feeling squeaky clean, but you actually don't want to strip away the natural protective layer on your skin. Don't scrub too hard, since that can irritate the skin and aggravate acne. Moisturize your skin every night with products that contain vitamin A, vitamin C, and vitamin E. Remove the dead skin by exfoliating gently each week. Healthy skin choices—which include protecting yourself from UV exposure—will give you vibrant skin and prevent damage that could lead to health consequences now and later in life.

Glossary

adjuvant therapy The treatment offered after primary cancer treatment in order to prevent the spread or recurrence of cancer.

basal cell carcinoma (BCC) A type of skin cancer that arises at the base of the epidermis; it is the most common form of skin cancer.

biopsy The removal of a sample of tissue from the body.

cancer A condition in which cells in the body undergo uncontrolled division and growth, in some cases disrupting and destroying normal body tissue.

carcinogen A chemical agent or other toxin that causes cancer.

dermatologist A doctor that specializes in diagnosing and treating skin conditions.

dermis The middle layer of the skin located beneath the epidermis.

DNA (deoxyribonucleic acid) The arrangement of bio-chemicals in a two-stranded chain that carries genetic information.

epidermis The outer layer of the skin.

gland A cell, group of cells, or organ that produces sub-stances used elsewhere in the body.

immune system The system of the body that fights infection and disease.

malignant Cancerous.

melanin A dark brown pigment in the skin produced by melanocytes.

melanocyte A cell primarily located in the epidermis that produces melanin.

melanoma A type of skin cancer that arises from melanocytes in the skin.

oncologist A doctor specializing in studying, diagnosing, and treating cancer.

psoriasis An autoimmune skin condition characterized by scaly red patches.

squamous cell carcinoma (SCC) A type of skin cancer that arises in cells of the epidermis; it is the second most common form of skin cancer.

sunblock An agent applied to the skin that reflects ultraviolet radiation.

sunscreen An agent applied to the skin that prevents ultraviolet radiation from penetrating the skin.

ultraviolet radiation (UVR) The wavelengths of light that tan and burn the skin.

vitiligo A medical condition in which patches of skin lose pigmentation.

For More Information

American Academy of Dermatology (AAD)
1350 I Street NW, Suite 880
Washington, DC 2005
(202) 842-3555
Web site: http://www.aad.org
  This nonprofit organization of dermatologists is committed
  to excellence in patient care, medical and public
  education, research, professionalism, and member
  service and support.

American Cancer Society (ACS)
American Cancer Society National Home Office
1599 Clifton Road
Atlanta, GA 30329
(800) 227-2345
Web site: http://www.cancer.org
  This nonprofit organization supports cancer research and
  provides educational materials.

Canadian Dermatology Association (CDA)
1385 Bank Street, Suite 425
Ottawa, ON K1H 8N4
Canada
(800) 267-3376

Web site: http://www.dermatology.ca
  The Canadian Dermatology Association is an organization
  that represents dermatologists in Canada.

Canadian Skin Cancer Foundation
780, 10665 Jasper Avenue
Edmonton, AB T5J 3S9
Canada
(780) 423-2723
Web site: http://www.canadianskincancer.com
  This foundation promotes education for awareness, prevention
  strategies, and early detection of skin cancer.

Skin Cancer Foundation
245 5th Avenue, Suite 1403
New York, NY 10016
(800) 754-6490
Web site: http://www.skincancer.org
  This nonprofit organization provides information on skin
  cancer and lists medical providers.

U.S. Department of Health and Human Services (HHS)
200 Independence Avenue SW
Washington, DC 20201
(877) 696-6775
Web site: http://www.hhs.gov
  This government agency is charged with protecting the health
  of all Americans and providing essential human services.

U.S. Food and Drug Administration (FDA)
10903 New Hampshire Avenue
Silver Spring, MD 20903
(888) 463-6332
Web site: http://www.fda.gov
This governmental organization is charged with protecting
public health in matters concerning food and medicine.

Web Sites

Due to the changing nature of Internet links, Rosen Publishing
has developed an online list of Web sites related to the subject
of this book. This site is updated regularly. Please use this link
to access the list:

http://www.rosenlinks.com/faq/tan

For Further Reading

Barrow, Mary Mills, and John F. Barrow. *Sun Protection for Life: Your Guide to a Lifetime of Healthy and Beautiful Skin*. Oakland, CA: New Harbinger Publications, Inc., 2005.

Beale, Lucy. *The Complete Idiot's Guide to Better Skin*. Indianapolis, IN: Alpha, 2004.

Close, Barbara. *Pure Skin: Organic Beauty Basics*. San Francisco, CA: Chronicle Books, 2005.

Donovan, Sandy. *Stay Clear: What You Should Know About Skin Care*. Minneapolis, MN: Lerner Publications Company, 2009.

Eby, Myra Michelle. *Return to Beautiful Skin: Your Guide to Truly Effective Nontoxic Skin Care*. Laguna Beach, CA: Basic Health Publications, 2008.

Eldridge, Lynne, M.D., and David Borgeson, M.S., MS, MPT. *Avoiding Cancer One Day at a Time: Practical Advice for Preventing Cancer*. Edina, MN: Beaver Pond Press, 2007.

Kunin, Audrey, M.D., with Bill Gottlieb. *The DERMAdoctor Skinstruction Manual: The Smart Guide to Healthy, Beautiful Skin and Looking Good at Any Age*. New York, NY: Simon & Schuster, 2005.

Poole, Catherine M. *Melanoma: Prevention, Detection, and Treatment*. Second Edition. New Haven, CT: Yale University Press, 2005.

Roizen, Michael F., M.D., and Mehmet C. Oz, M.D. *You, Being Beautiful: The Owner's Manual to Inner and Outer Beauty.* New York, NY: Free Press, 2008.

Schofield, Jill R., M.D., and William A. Robinson, M.D., Ph.D. *What You Really Need to Know About Moles and Melanoma.* Baltimore, MD: Johns Hopkins University Press, 2000.

Simons, Rae. *For All to See: A Teen's Guide to Healthy Skin.* Philadelphia, PA: Mason Crest Publishers, 2004.

So, Po-lin, Ph.D. *Skin Cancer.* New York, NY: Chelsea House Publishing, 2007.

About the Author

Corona Brezina has written more than a dozen titles for Rosen Publishing. Several of her previous books have also focused on health and wellness issues, including *Death of a Friend* (Teen Health and Wellness). She lives in Chicago.

Photo Credits

Cover © www.istockphoto.com/Dušan Zidar; p. 5 © www.istockphoto.com/Stephan Hoerold; p. 7 © www.istockphoto.com/Bora Ucak; p. 9 © www.istockphoto.com/David H. Lewis; p. 13 © www.istockphoto.com/Graça Victoria; p. 16 © www.istockphoto.com/Ezequiel Casares; p. 18 © www.istockphoto.com/Alison Hess; p. 24 © Michel Gilles/Photo Researchers; p. 26 www.istockphoto.com; p. 30 © www.istockphoto.com; p. 35 © Dr. P. Marazzi/Photo Researchers; p. 37 © BSIP/Photo Researchers; p. 39 © Custom Medical Stock Photo; p. 42 www.istockphoto.com/Khuong Hoang; p. 48 © www.istockphoto.com/Franck Camhi; p. 51 © Phanie/Photo Researchers; p. 53 © www.istockphoto.com/Chris Schmidt.

Designer: Nicole Russo; Editor: Nicholas Croce;
Photo Researcher: Marty Levick